Places to See

by Quinn Baker

This is a desert.
What can you see?

See the cactus with yellow flowers.

This is a mountain.
What can you see?

See the mountain goat on the rock.

This is a city.
What can you see?

See the yellow taxi on the street.

This is the ocean.
See the fish.

Do they see you?